LIVING ON THE EDGE™

SO-BAH-083

FREE ACCESS TO VIDEO TEACHING

You can stream it for FREE by following the directions below.
Or you can order a DVD at (888) 333-6003 or
LivingontheEdge.org.

YOUR ONLINE CODE

7379052-6KY2-3365

🌐 Please visit LivingontheEdge.org/access and enter this code.

---

3 EASY STEPS

1 **CREATE AN ACCOUNT**
Go to LivingontheEdge.org/access and complete
the steps to create your FREE account.

2 **GET IMMEDIATE ACCESS**
Now you will be connected to the resources which
will be needed throughout this workbook.

3 **ACCESS ANYTIME**
• Log back into your account anytime by visiting
LivingontheEdge.org and click on STORE.
• From the STORE page, click on Login/Register.
• Enter your login information. Once you are in your
account, click on MEMBERSHIPS.

Real Heaven

LIVING™
ON THE EDGE
BIBLE STUDY

THE
REAL
HEAVEN

What the Bible Actually Says

CHIPINGRAM

WITH LANCE WITT

THE
REAL
HEAVEN

What the Bible Actually Says

 **LIVING** ON THE EDGE | **Helping Christians Live Like Christians** LivingontheEdge.org

Table of Contents

How to Start Your Own Small Group

The fact that you are even reading this page says a lot about you. It says that you are either one of those people that has to read everything, or it says you are open to God using you to lead a group.

Leading a small group can sound intimidating, but it really doesn't have to be. Think of it more as gathering a few friends to get to know each other better and to have some discussion around spiritual matters.

Here are a few practical tips to help you get started:

1. Pray — One of the most important principles of spiritual leadership is to realize you can't do this on your own. No matter how long you've been a Christian or been involved in ministry, you need the power of the Holy Spirit. Lean on Him; He will help you.

2. Invite some friends — Don't be afraid to ask people to come to your group. You will be surprised how many people are open to a study like this. Whether you have 4 or 14 in your group, it can be a powerful experience. You should probably plan on at least an hour and a half for your group meeting.

3. Get your materials — You will need to use the streaming code in the front of each study guide or You can get the DVD from LivingontheEdge.org. It will also be helpful for each person to have their own study guide. You can also purchase those through the Website as well.

4. Be prepared to facilitate — Just a few minutes a week in preparation can make a huge difference in the group experience. Each week, preview the video teaching and review the discussion questions. If you don't think your group can get through all the questions, select the ones that are most relevant to your group.

5. Learn to say, "I don't know" — When tough questions come up, it's OK for you to say "I don't know." Take the pressure off. No one expects you to have all the answers.

6. Love your group — Maybe the most important thing you bring to the group is your personal care for them. If you will pray for them, encourage them, call them, email them, involve them, and love them, God will be pleased and you will have a lot of fun along the way.

Thank you for your availability. May God bless you as you serve Him by serving others.

How to Get the Most Out of This Experience

There is a lot of confusion and misconception about Heaven. Most of our ideas about Heaven come more from Hollywood than they do from Scripture. During this series Chip Ingram will lead us to discover what God says about the place He is preparing for us.

Listed below are the segments you will experience each week as well as some hints for getting the most out of this experience. If you are leading the group, you will find some additional help and coaching on pages 53-63.

Take It In (Watch the Video)

It is important for us to get before God and submit ourselves to His truth. During this section, you will watch the video teaching by Chip. He will introduce each session with a personal word to the group, followed by the teaching portion of the video. At the end of the teaching segment, Chip will wrap up the session and help the group dive into discussion.

A teaching outline with fill-ins is provided for each session. As you follow along, write down questions or insights that you can share during the discussion time.

Even though most of the verses will appear on the screen and in your notes, it is a great idea to bring your own Bible each week. It will allow you to make notes in your own Bible and find other passages that might be relevant to that week's study.

Talk It Over

We not only grow by listening to God's Word, but we grow in community. The friendship and insights of those in the group will enrich your small group experience. Several discussion questions are provided for your group to further engage in the teaching content. Keep the following guidelines in mind for having a healthy group discussion.

- Be involved. Jump in and share your thoughts. Your ideas are important, and you have a perspective that is unique and can benefit the other group members.

- Be a good listener. Value what others are sharing. Seek to really understand the perspectives of others in your group, and don't be afraid to ask follow-up questions.

- Be courteous. People hold strong opinions about the topics in this study. Spirited discussion is great; disrespect and attack is not. When there is disagreement, focus on the issue and never turn the discussion into a personal attack.

- Be focused. Stay on topic. Help the group explore the subject at hand, and try to save unrelated questions or stories for afterwards.

- Be careful not to dominate. Be aware of the amount of talking you are doing in proportion to the rest of the group, and make space for others to speak.

- Be a learner. Stay sensitive to what God might be wanting to teach you through the lesson, as well as through what others have to say. Focus more on your own growth rather than making a point or winning an argument.

Live It Out – B.I.O.

Bio is a word that is synonymous with "life." Found in those three simple letters B.I.O. is the key to helping you become the person God wants you to be.

B = Come "Before God" daily - Meet with Him personally through prayer and His Word to enjoy His presence, receive His direction, and follow His will.

I = Do Life "In Community" weekly - Structure your week to personally connect in safe relationships that provide love, support, transparency, challenge, and accountability.

O = Be "On Mission" 24/7 - Cultivate a mindset to live out Jesus' love for others through acts of sacrifice as well as service at home, work, play, and church.

Accelerate (20 minutes that turn concepts into convictions)

Inspiration comes from hearing God's Word. **Motivation** grows by discussing God's Word. **Transformation** occurs when you study it for yourself.

If you want to "accelerate" your growth, there is an assignment you can do at home each week. Our convictions become even stronger when we dig into Scripture and discover truth for ourselves. To help you get the most out of this exercise, consider partnering up with someone in your group who will also commit to doing the assignment this week. Then, after you have each completed the assignment, agree to spend 10 minutes by phone sharing what you learned and what you are applying.

Session 1
Why Heaven Matters
Part 1

Take It In (Watch the Video)

Why Study Heaven?

1. Our misconceptions are crippling us:

   • Common misconceptions.

   • Predictable results.

2. We're commanded to do so.

   Therefore, if you have been raised up with Christ, keep seeking the things above, where Christ is, seated at the right hand of God. Set your mind on the things above, not on the things that are on earth. For you have died and your life is hidden with Christ in God. When Christ, who is our life, is revealed, then you also will be revealed with Him in glory.

   COLOSSIANS 3:1-4 (NASB)

3. A faulty view of Heaven destines us to a wasted life on earth.

   Do not let your heart be troubled; believe in God, believe also in Me. In My Father's house are many dwelling places; if it were not so, I would have told you; for I go to prepare a place for you. If I go and prepare a place for you, I will come again and receive you to Myself, that where I am, there you may be also.

   JOHN 14:1-3 (NASB)

I. A Theology of Heaven

• Definition – Three uses of the word.

• The Promise of Heaven:

   - It's a real, tangible place (John 14)

   - The Father is there (Matthew 6:9)

   - Jesus is at His right hand (Hebrews 9:24)

- Believing loved ones are there (Hebrews 12:23)
- Our names are recorded there (Luke 10:20)
- We have an inheritance there (1 Peter 1:4)
- Our citizenship is there (Philippians 3:20)
- Specific, eternal rewards are given (Matthew 6:19-21)
- It's the best of earth…better (Revelation 22)
- Sin, death, and sorrow are absent (Revelation 22)
- Adventure, work, discovery, and rulership await us (Revelation 22)

- Heaven in historical context:
  1. Past – Eden (Genesis 1-2)
  2. Present – Intermediate Heaven (Genesis 3 - Revelation 20)
  3. Future – New Heaven and New Earth (Revelation 22)

Talk It Over

1. When you walked into this study today, what was your image of Heaven?

   _____

   _____

   _____

2. How did this first session shift your understanding of Heaven?

   _____

   _____

   _____

3. In the early centuries of the Church, Heaven was a common topic of conversation, sermons, and songs. Why do you think that in the modern Church Heaven is rarely talked about?

   _____

   _____

   _____

4. Chip said, "a faulty view of Heaven destines us to a wasted life on earth."
    How would a faulty view of Heaven diminish our life on earth?

    _____

    _____

    _____

Live It Out – B.I.O.

Bio is a word that is synonymous with "life." Found in those three simple letters —
B.I.O. — is the key to helping you become the person God wants you to be.

B = COME "BEFORE GOD" DAILY
Meet with Him personally through prayer and His Word to enjoy His
presence, receive His direction, and follow His will.

I = DO LIFE "IN COMMUNITY" WEEKLY
Structure your week to personally connect in safe relationships that provide
love, support, transparency, challenge, and accountability.

O = BE "ON MISSION" 24/7
Cultivate a mindset to live out Jesus' love for others through acts of sacrifice
as well as service at home, work, play, and church.

Come Before God

5. In Romans 12:1-2 (NIV), Paul says:

    Therefore, I urge you, brothers and sisters, in view of God's mercy,
    to offer your bodies as a living sacrifice, holy and pleasing to God—
    this is your true and proper worship. Do not conform to the pattern
    of this world, but be transformed by the renewing of your mind.
    Then you will be able to test and approve what God's will is—his
    good, pleasing and perfect will.

Chip said Satan is the father of lies who keeps us focused on a world system that he's behind. In what ways does the modern world system distract us from thinking about Heaven?

_____

_____

_____

Do Life In Community

6. What are some practical ways that we could help one another to be more "Heavenly minded"?

_____

_____

_____

Be On Mission

7. How would a clear view of Heaven help us be "On Mission" for God?

_____

_____

_____

Accelerate (20 minutes that turn concepts into convictions)

Inspiration comes from hearing God's Word. **Motivation** grows by discussing God's Word. **Transformation** occurs when you study it for yourself.

If you want to "accelerate" your growth, here is an assignment you can do at home each week. Our convictions become even stronger when we dig into Scripture and discover truth for ourselves. To help you get the most out of this exercise, consider partnering up with someone in your group who will also commit to doing the assignment this week. Then, after you have each completed the assignment, agree to spend 10 minutes by phone sharing what you learned and what you are applying.

Come Before God

1. Read the following passage carefully and slowly.

   Since, then, you have been raised with Christ, set your hearts on things above, where Christ is, seated at the right hand of God. Set your minds on things above, not on earthly things. For you died, and your life is now hidden with Christ in God. When Christ, who is your life, appears, then you also will appear with him in glory.

   COLOSSIANS 3:1-4 (NIV)

2. Twice in this passage, Paul commands us to set our hearts and minds on things above. Why do you think he ties this command to Christ being raised and Christ being seated at the right hand of God?

   _____

   _____

   _____

3. In verse 3, Paul states that our "life is now hidden in Christ." Do a search in your Bible of the phrase "in Christ." Then, look up some of those verses in the New Testament and discover your identity "in Christ."

4. In Matthew 6:19-21 (NIV) Jesus said:

   Do not store up for yourselves treasures on earth, where moths and vermin destroy, and where thieves break in and steal. But store up for yourselves treasures in Heaven, where moths and vermin do not destroy, and where thieves do not break in and steal. For where your treasure is, there your heart will be also.

From this passage, what is the downside of storing up treasures on earth? For you personally, what would need to change for you to store up more treasures in Heaven?

_____

_____

_____

Do Life In Community

5. Have a conversation with your spouse or a friend about setting your heart on things above. Discuss what it would look like for you to "set your heart on things above, not on earthly things."

Be On Mission

6. How would setting your heart "on things above" change how you view your neighbor, co-worker, and unbelieving friends? Spend a few moments right now praying for an unbelieving friend. Ask God to give you an opportunity to share the gospel with them.

Session 2
Why Heaven Matters
Part 2

Take It In (Watch the Video)

Heaven in historical context:

1. Past – Eden (Genesis 1-2)

2. Present – Intermediate Heaven (Genesis 3 - Revelation 20)

3. Future – New Heaven and New Earth (Revelation 21-22)

Genesis 1 and 2:

> *Then God said, "Let Us make man in Our image, according to Our likeness; and let them rule over the fish of the sea and over the birds of the sky and over the cattle and over all the earth, and over every creeping thing that creeps on the earth." God created man in His own image, in the image of God He created him; male and female He created them.*

> **GENESIS 1:26-27 (NASB)**

> *When the woman saw that the tree was good for food, and that it was a delight to the eyes, and that the tree was desirable to make one wise, she took from its fruit and ate; and she gave also to her husband with her, and he ate. Then the eyes of both of them were opened, and they knew that they were naked; and they sewed fig leaves together and made themselves loin coverings.*

> *They heard the sound of the LORD God walking in the garden in the cool of the day, and the man and his wife hid themselves from the presence of the LORD God among the trees of the garden. Then the LORD God called to the man, and said to him, "Where are you?" He said, "I heard the sound of You in the garden, and I was afraid because I was naked; so I hid myself."*

> **GENESIS 3:6-10 (NASB)**

The LORD God made garments of skin for Adam and his wife, and clothed them. Then the LORD God said, "Behold, the man has become like one of Us, knowing good and evil; and now, he might stretch out his hand, and take also from the tree of life, and eat, and live forever"

GENESIS 3:21-22 (NASB)

Then I saw a New Heaven and a New Earth; for the first Heaven and the first earth passed away, and there is no longer any sea. And I saw the holy city, new Jerusalem, coming down out of Heaven from God, made ready as a bride adorned for her husband. And I heard a loud voice from the throne, saying, "Behold, the tabernacle of God is among men, and He will dwell among them, and they shall be His people, and God Himself will be among them, and He will wipe away every tear from their eyes; and there will no longer be any death; there will no longer be any mourning, or crying, or pain; the first things have passed away." And He who sits on the throne said, "Behold, I am making all things new." And He said, "Write, for these words are faithful and true."

REVELATION 21:1-5 (NASB)

II. **Understanding Heaven requires a macroscopic view of Scripture and a microscopic view of God's purpose for His people.**

MACRO VIEW OF SCRIPTURE

MICRO VIEW OF GOD'S RESPONSES

GOD	GOD	GOD	GOD
Genesis 1-2	Genesis 3 - Revelation 19	Revelation 20	Revelation 21-22
With Man in a Perfect Earth	Separated From Man in a Cursed Earth	With Man in a Temporary Earth	With Man in a Perfect Earth Forever

JESUS	JESUS	JESUS	JESUS
In Theophany Visits Earth	The Incarnate Savior and Redeemer	King of Kings	The Emmanuel Forever

God's Original Intent for Man on Earth

Sin, Death, Cursed Earth ⟶

Christ's Redemption and Promise of Resurrection to Make All Things New

God's New Heaven Comes Down on the New Earth

Summary – God wants to be with His people!

An Accurate View of Heaven Provides....

- Perspective in times of trouble (2 Corinthians 4):

> *But though our outer man is decaying, yet our inner man is being renewed day by day. For momentary, light affliction is producing for us an eternal weight of glory far beyond all comparison, while we look not at the things which are seen, but at the things which are not seen; for the things which are seen are temporal, but the things which are not seen are eternal.*

2 CORINTHIANS 4:16-18 (NASB)

- Perseverance in times of temptation (John 14)
- Priorities when under pressure (Matthew 6)

Talk It Over

1. An accurate view of Heaven provides...

   - Perspective in times of trouble

   - Perseverance in times of temptation

   - Priorities when under pressure

   Which one of those three statements most connects with you personally? Why?

   _____

   _____

   _____

2. How can one's view of Heaven help you in dealing with challenges and temptations?

   _____

   _____

   _____

3. What new insight did you gain about Heaven from this week's teaching?

   _____

   _____

   _____

4. Read Revelation 21:1-7. What one thing about the New Heaven and the New Earth most excites you? Why?

   _____

   _____

   _____

Live It Out – B.I.O.

Bio is a word that is synonymous with "life." Found in those three simple letters — B.I.O. — is the key to helping you become the person God wants you to be.

B = Come "Before God" daily
Meet with Him personally through prayer and His Word to enjoy His presence, receive His direction, and follow His will.

I = Do Life "In Community" weekly
Structure your week to personally connect in safe relationships that provide love, support, transparency, challenge, and accountability.

O = Be "On Mission" 24/7
Cultivate a mindset to live out Jesus' love for others through acts of sacrifice as well as service at home, work, play, and church.

Come Before God

5.   In 2 Corinthians 4:16-18 (NIV) Paul says:

Therefore we do not lose heart. Though outwardly we are wasting away, yet inwardly we are being renewed day by day. For our light and momentary troubles are achieving for us an eternal glory that far outweighs them all. So we fix our eyes not on what is seen, but on what is unseen, since what is seen is temporary, but what is unseen is eternal.

What does it mean that "inwardly we are being renewed day by day"?

_____

_____

_____

Do Life In Community

6.   In what ways could you help one another "not lose heart" and fix your eyes on "what is unseen"? Get practical!

_____

_____

_____

Be On Mission

7.   Heaven reminds us that this life is not all there is. All of us will spend eternity somewhere. Spend a few minutes as a group praying for friends, family, neighbors, and co-workers who don't know Christ and right now don't have the promise of a home in Heaven.

Accelerate (20 minutes that turn concepts into convictions)

Inspiration comes from hearing God's Word. **Motivation** grows by discussing God's Word. **Transformation** occurs when you study it for yourself.

If you want to "accelerate" your growth, here is an assignment you can do at home each week. Our convictions become even stronger when we dig into Scripture and discover truth for ourselves. To help you get the most out of this exercise, consider partnering up with someone in your group who will also commit to doing the assignment this week. Then, after you have each completed the assignment, agree to spend 10 minutes by phone sharing what you learned and what you are applying.

Come Before God

1. Read the following passage carefully and slowly.

   Therefore we do not lose heart. Though outwardly we are wasting away, yet inwardly we are being renewed day by day. For our light and momentary troubles are achieving for us an eternal glory that far outweighs them all. So we fix our eyes not on what is seen, but on what is unseen, since what is seen is temporary, but what is unseen is eternal.

   2 CORINTHIANS 4:16-18 (NIV)

2. Go through this passage and make a list of the words and phrases that are filled with hope and promise.

   - _____
   - _____
   - _____
   - _____
   - _____

3. The "unseen" is the presence of God and a place called Heaven. Read Revelation 21:1-4 to "see the unseen." What painful things does God promise to remove?

   _____
   _____
   _____

4. From the same passage in Revelation 21, what beautiful things does God add that are different from our experience here on earth?

    _____

    _____

    _____

Do Life In Community

5. Who do you know that might be comforted by the words of 2 Corinthians 4:16-18? Send them a card, email, or text message this week to encourage them.

Be On Mission

6. Read Revelation 21:7-8. Verse 8 is a sobering reminder that those who don't know Christ will spend an eternity in a place the Bible calls Hell. Who do you have a relationship with that needs to hear the gospel? Pray that God gives you a sense of urgency and the opportunity to share the good news with that person.

Session 3
What's Heaven Like?
Part 1

THE
REAL
HEAVEN
What the Bible Actually Says

Take It In (Watch the Video)

Introduction – What's your idea of Heaven?

Review – A Biblical overview of Heaven

PAST Genesis 1-2	PRESENT Genesis 3 - Revelation 19	FUTURE Revelation 20-22
Original Mankind	Fallen Mankind; Some Believe and Are Transformed	Resurrected Mankind
Original Earth	Fallen Earth with Glimmers of Original	New Earth; Resurrected on Mankind's Coattails
God Deligates Earth's Reign to Innocent Mankind	Disputed Reign with God, Satan, and Fallen Mankind	God Deligates Earth's Reign to Righteous Mankind
Creation and Mankind Perfect	Creation and Mankind Tainted by Sin	Creation and Mankind Restored to Perfection
Mankind in Ideal Place	Mankind Banished, Struggles, and Wanders in Fallen Places	Mankind Restored to Ideal Place, but Much Improved
God's Plan for Mankind and Earth Revealed	God's Plan for Mankind and Earth Delayed and Enriched	God's Plan for Mankind and Earth Realized

From Randy Alcorn's Book

Question – What's Heaven like?

I. What will Heaven be like if you died today? (Revelation 4-20)

One minute after a <u>believer</u> dies...

- Angels usher your soul to Heaven (Luke 16:22)

- You immediately enter God's presence (2 Corinthians 5:6-8)

- You are conscious, in command of your faculties of thinking, feeling, speech, and memories (Luke 16:19-31)

- You participate in magnificent worship with angels and believers before the throne of God and Christ (Revelation 4-5)

- You are aware to some degree of activities and events on Earth (Revelation 6:9-10)

- You will recognize and communicate with believers who preceded you to Heaven (Luke 9:28-36)

Talk It Over

1. What are you learning about Heaven that gives you the most comfort and hope?

   _____

   _____

   _____

2. From Chip's teaching, what new fact about Heaven most surprised you? Why?

   _____

   _____

   _____

3. Review Revelation 4:1-11 and 5:11-14. What can we learn from this scene of majestic worship that should inform how we worship in this life?

   _____

   _____

   _____

4. Read Luke 9:28-36. What can we learn from this passage about our identity, bodies, and communication in Heaven?

    _____

    _____

    _____

Live It Out – B.I.O.

Bio is a word that is synonymous with "life." Found in those three simple letters — B.I.O. — is the key to helping you become the person God wants you to be.

B = Come "Before God" daily
Meet with Him personally through prayer and His Word to enjoy His presence, receive His direction, and follow His will.

I = Do Life "In Community" weekly
Structure your week to personally connect in safe relationships that provide love, support, transparency, challenge, and accountability.

O = Be "On Mission" 24/7
Cultivate a mindset to live out Jesus' love for others through acts of sacrifice as well as service at home, work, play, and church.

Come Before God

5. Read Luke 16:19-31. What can we learn from this sobering passage about Heaven, Hell, and God's judgment?

    _____

    _____

    _____

Do Life In Community

6. Heaven is a relational place. Who is one person that you are looking forward to spending time with in Heaven? Why? It could be someone you know that has gone on to be with the Lord or it could be someone from the Bible or history that was a believer.

    _____

    _____

    _____

Be On Mission

7. Just as there is a real eternal place called Heaven, the Bible declares there is a real eternal place called Hell. If you lived with a greater awareness of the horrible reality of Hell, how might that change you?

    _____

    _____

    _____

Accelerate (20 minutes that turn concepts into convictions)

Inspiration comes from hearing God's Word. **Motivation** grows by discussing God's Word. **Transformation** occurs when you study it for yourself.

If you want to "accelerate" your growth, here is an assignment you can do at home each week. Our convictions become even stronger when we dig into Scripture and discover truth for ourselves. To help you get the most out of this exercise, consider partnering up with someone in your group who will also commit to doing the assignment this week. Then, after you have each completed the assignment, agree to spend 10 minutes by phone sharing what you learned and what you are applying.

Come Before God

1. This week read Revelation 4-5 several times.

2. Try to imagine what it would be like to witness that majestic worship service. What most stands out to you from this scene? Why?

   _____

   _____

   _____

3. Make a list of the qualities and characteristics of worship that you see in this passage.

   _____

   _____

   _____

4. In Revelation 4 and 5, how is Jesus pictured differently than how you see Him in the gospels?

   _____

   _____

   _____

Do Life In Community

5. Have a conversation with a friend or family member this week about worship. What can you do that would take your worship to a whole new level?

   _____

   _____

   _____

Be On Mission

6. Take the risk this week to have a conversation with someone about "life after death." Ask them what they believe happens to us when we die? It will give you an opportunity to share what you are learning from this study.

_____

_____

_____

Session 4

What's Heaven Like?

Part 2

THE
REAL
HEAVEN

What the Bible Actually Says

Take It In (Watch the Video)

What will Heaven be like if you died today?

- You will be joined by all living Christians when Jesus "Raptures" the Church from the Earth to be judged for rewards at the Bema Seat. You will then enjoy the Marriage Supper of the Lamb in Heaven with Christ and His Bride. (2 Corinthians 5:10, Revelation 19:6-10)

- You will await God's judgment of the Earth at the end of the Tribulation and will be bodily resurrected to reign and judge with Christ for 1,000 years on the Earth. (Revelation 20:4-6)

- You will witness the justice of God at the judgment of Satan, angels, and the wicked dead at the Great White Throne. (Revelation 20:11-15)

- You will witness the New Heaven coming down on the New Earth. (Revelation 21:1)

II. **What will Heaven be like in the New Heaven and the New Earth?** — Revelation 21-22

- It will be a lot like the "New_____."

- Just as my body will be _____,so the Earth will be

  _____. (1 Corinthians 15:40-53)

- My new body will be like _____. (1 John 3:2-3)

- Jesus' resurrected body _____ and _____, had flesh and bone and new capabilities. (Luke 24:39)

- It will be a lot like the Old _____.

- The New Heaven and New Earth is _____. (Revelation 21:1)

- The Old Earth "passes away" not _____. (2 Peter 3:8-9)

- Like the "Old Me" passed away, so will the Old _____ . (2 Corinthians 5:17)

- The New Earth = New, better, different, but with continuity from the Old Earth.

Summary

As Man was, so was the Earth,

As Man went, so went the Earth,

As Man will be, so will be the Earth.

Talk It Over

1. What if you were the apostle John and God gave you the experience of seeing into Heaven? How do you think it would change you?

   _____

   _____

   _____

2. Chip talked about the judgment of believers called the Judgment Seat of Christ (2 Corinthians 5:10). 1 Corinthians 3:10-15 gives a more thorough description of this judgment. Discuss the passage in 1 Corinthians 3 and share insights that you observe about this judgment of believers.

3. From 1 Corinthians 3, what is the significance of the difference between gold, silver, and precious stones and wood, hay, and straw?

   _____

   _____

   _____

4. From Chip's description of the New Heaven and the New Earth, what is most surprising to you?

_____

_____

_____

Live It Out – B.I.O.

Bio is a word that is synonymous with "life." Found in those three simple letters — B.I.O. — is the key to helping you become the person God wants you to be.

B = Come "Before God" daily
Meet with Him personally through prayer and His Word to enjoy His presence, receive His direction, and follow His will.

I = Do Life "In Community" weekly
Structure your week to personally connect in safe relationships that provide love, support, transparency, challenge, and accountability.

O = Be "On Mission" 24/7
Cultivate a mindset to live out Jesus' love for others through acts of sacrifice as well as service at home, work, play, and church.

Come Before God

5. Read Revelation 20:1-6 which describes the Millennium. Remember, this is the 1,000 year reign of Christ on the earth after the Rapture. From this passage, what most stands out to you about the Millennium?

_____

_____

_____

Do Life In Community

6. Since we will all be there together at the Marriage Supper of the Lamb, what if your group were in charge of planning the wedding celebration? What would this great party look like?

_____

_____

_____

Be On Mission

7. Read Revelation 20:11-15 and then spend some time in prayer as a group asking God to give you a heart to reach those who are without Christ.

Accelerate (20 minutes that turn concepts into convictions)

Inspiration comes from hearing God's Word. **Motivation** grows by discussing God's Word. **Transformation** occurs when you study it for yourself.

If you want to "accelerate" your growth, here is an assignment you can do at home each week. Our convictions become even stronger when we dig into Scripture and discover truth for ourselves. To help you get the most out of this exercise, consider partnering up with someone in your group who will also commit to doing the assignment this week. Then, after you have each completed the assignment, agree to spend 10 minutes by phone sharing what you learned and what you are applying.

Come Before God

1. Carefully and slowly read 1 Corinthians 3:10-15.

2. In verse 10, Paul says that each of us "should build with care." What do you think he means by that statement?

_____

_____

_____

3. Verse 13 says that the quality of our works will be tested with fire. What kinds of works won't survive the fire?

    _____

    _____

    _____

4. In verse 15, Paul says that if the works are burned up, the builder will "suffer loss." If this is a judgment of believers and is a judgment of rewards, what does it mean that they will "suffer loss"?

    _____

    _____

    _____

Do Life In Community

5. Sit down this week with someone from your small group and have a discussion about the Judgment Seat of Christ. Discuss how you are doing these days with storing up treasures in Heaven and preparing for this coming Judgment of Rewards.

Be On Mission

6. Read Revelation 20:11-15 a few times this week. Let the sobering reality of the Great White Throne Judgment sit with you this week. Ask God to give you greater urgency for sharing the gospel.

Session 5

A New Home for the New You

Part 1

THE
REAL
HEAVEN

What the Bible Actually Says

THE **REAL HEAVEN**
What the Bible Actually Says

Take It In (Watch the video)

Intro – Have You Ever Wondered...

1. Will Heaven be an actual place?

2. What will we look like in Heaven?

3. Will Heaven be boring?

4. What will we do for all eternity?

5. Will animals be in Heaven?

6. Where will we live in Heaven?

7. Who gets to go to Heaven?

FIRST EARTH (EDEN) Genesis 1-2	FALLEN EARTH (NOW) Genesis 3 - Revelation 20	NEW EARTH (HEAVEN) Revelation 21-22
Original Mankind	Christ Restores Mankind	God Lives with Man Forever
Perfect Environment	Creation Groans (Tornadoes, Tsunamis, Etc.)	Restored Environment
No Sin	Sin and Death	No Sin or Death Ever

What Will Heaven Be Like on the New Earth?

1. It will be a lot like the new me.

   • A _____ Body (1 Corinthians 15:42-49)

   • A _____ Earth (Isaiah 65:17, 2 Peter 3:9-13)

2. It will be a lot like the first earth. (Genesis 1-2)

   - A perfect environment
   - A Tree of Life
   - A river, trees, fruit, food
   - Animals, harmony, peace, beauty
   - No death, no shame, no curse
   - No sin, no sorrow, no pain
   - Meaningful work to accomplish
   - Intimacy with God and people

3. It will be a lot different and infinitely better because we will have: (Revelation 21-22)

   - A new kind of relationship with _____. (1-3)

   - A new kind of relationship with _____. (4-5)

   - A new kind of experience of complete _____. (6-8)

   - A new city and people to _____. (9-23)

   - A New Earth with new _____, commerce,

     culture, and capabilities and love our God.

     (Revelation 21:9 – 22:5)

Summary = Behold I will make all things _____!

(Revelation 21:5)

Talk It Over

1. Share about a time in your life when you really "thirsted" for (wanted) something...and when you got it, it just didn't satisfy like you thought it would.

2. Chip said that the New Earth is a lot like the old earth... but better. What do you love about this earth that you would be excited to have in the New Earth?

   _____

   _____

   _____

3. What intrigues you the most or what questions do you have about the "glorified" body you will have in Heaven?

   _____

   _____

   _____

4. In Heaven, we will have a new kind of relationship with God. As a group, make a list of ways that our relationship with God will be different in Heaven than it is here in this life.

   _____

   _____

   _____

Live It Out – B.I.O.

Bio is a word that is synonymous with "life." Found in those three simple letters — B.I.O. — is the key to helping you become the person God wants you to be.

B = Come "Before God" daily
Meet with Him personally through prayer and His Word to enjoy His presence, receive His direction, and follow His will.

I = Do Life "In Community" weekly
Structure your week to personally connect in safe relationships that provide love, support, transparency, challenge, and accountability.

O = Be "On Mission" 24/7
Cultivate a mindset to live out Jesus' love for others through acts of sacrifice as well as service at home, work, play, and church.

Come Before God

5. Read 2 Peter 3:9-13. What can we learn from this passage about the Lord's return and the establishment of the New Heaven and the New Earth?

    _____

    _____

    _____

Do Life In Community

6. Chip said that in Heaven we will have total and "complete satisfaction." A lot of the things we struggle with in this life, we won't struggle with in Heaven. What is one thing in your life or past that you are glad you won't have to deal with in Heaven?

    _____

    _____

    _____

Be On Mission

7. In 2 Peter 3, the Bible says God is patient towards mankind "not wishing for any to perish, but for all to come to repentance." What other verses can you think of that portray God's compassion and love for unbelievers?

_____

_____

_____

Accelerate (20 minutes that turn concepts into convictions)

Inspiration comes from hearing God's Word. **Motivation** grows by discussing God's Word. **Transformation** occurs when you study it for yourself.

If you want to "accelerate" your growth, here is an assignment you can do at home each week. Our convictions become even stronger when we dig into Scripture and discover truth for ourselves. To help you get the most out of this exercise, consider partnering up with someone in your group who will also commit to doing the assignment this week. Then, after you have each completed the assignment, agree to spend 10 minutes by phone sharing what you learned and what you are applying.

Come Before God

1. Read 1 Corinthians 15:35-58.

2. From this passage, make a list of some of the qualities/descriptions of our future glorified body.

_____

_____

_____

3. What does Paul mean in verse 43 that our natural body is "sown in dishonor"?

_____

_____

_____

4. Why is Jesus referred to as the "last Adam"? You might have to find a commentary or look online for a good theological explanation.

_____

_____

_____

Do Life In Community

5. Verses 54-56 speak of Christ's victory over death, and therefore, our victory over death. Is there someone you know that is going through a time of grief or loss that could use the encouragement of this passage? Send them a card or an email and share these verses with them.

Be On Mission

6. 1 Corinthians 15:58 (NIV) says:

Therefore, my dear brothers and sisters, stand firm. Let nothing move you. Always give yourselves fully to the work of the Lord, because you know that your labor in the Lord is not in vain.

Why does Paul connect the teaching about the glorified body to a challenge to give ourselves fully to the work of the Lord?

_____

_____

_____

Session 6

A New Home for the New You

Part 2

Take It In (Watch the Video)

Heaven will be a lot different and infinitely better because we will have...
(Revelation 21-22)

Review from Session 5

- A new kind of relationship with _____ . (1-3)

- A new kind of relationship with _____ . (4-5)

- A new kind of experience of complete _____ . (6-8)

- A New City and people to _____ . (9-23)

- A New Earth with New _____ , commerce,

  culture, and capabilities and love our God.

  (Revelations 21:9 – 22:5)

Summary = Behold I will make all things new! (Revelation 21:5)

Talk It Over

1. Since receiving Christ is the only way to get to Heaven, start your group discussion this week by having two or three of you share briefly about how you came to Christ.

2. What adjustments do you need to make to your current priorities and passions to have a more eternal perspective?

   _____

   _____

   _____

3. Review Revelation 21:9-27. What is most striking to you about this description of Heaven? What are some things that won't be in the New Heaven and New Earth?

_____

_____

_____

4. Revelation 22:7 says that we will "reign forever and ever." What do you think that looks like practically?

_____

_____

_____

Live It Out – B.I.O.

Bio is a word that is synonymous with "life." Found in those three simple letters — B.I.O. — is the key to helping you become the person God wants you to be.

B = Come "Before God" daily
Meet with Him personally through prayer and His word to enjoy His presence, receive His direction, and follow His will.

I = Do Life "In Community" weekly
Structure your week to personally connect in safe relationships that provide love, support, transparency, challenge, and accountability.

O = Be "On Mission" 24/7
Cultivate a mindset to live out Jesus' love for others through acts of sacrifice as well as service at home, work, play, and church.

Come Before God

5. Review Revelation 22:1-5. What can we learn about Heaven from these 5 verses?

_____

_____

_____

Do Life In Community

6. When John saw this magnificent Revelation of Heaven, he fell down at the feet of the angel who gave him this glimpse of Heaven. But the angel says, "Don't worship me... worship God."

    As you think about what you've learned about Heaven, share with each other how this makes you love and worship God more.

Be On Mission

7. Is there someone you care about that doesn't know about Heaven or how to get there? How could God use you to help him or her?

    _____

    _____

    _____

Accelerate (20 minutes that turn concepts into convictions)

Inspiration comes from hearing God's Word. **Motivation** grows by discussing God's Word. **Transformation** occurs when you study it for yourself.

If you want to "accelerate" your growth, here is an assignment you can do at home each week. Our convictions become even stronger when we dig into Scripture and discover truth for ourselves. To help you get the most out of this exercise, consider partnering up with someone in your group who will also commit to doing the assignment this week. Then, after you have each completed the assignment, agree to spend 10 minutes by phone sharing what you learned and what you are applying.

Come Before God

1. Read Revelation 21 and 22.

2. What is the image of the bride (Rev. 21:2,9) and why is it a fitting portrayal of Heaven?

    _____

    _____

    _____

3. What are some characteristics of God that you observe in Revelation 21 and 22?

    _____

    _____

    _____

4. From Revelation 21 and 22, make a list of some of the activities that takes place.

    _____

    _____

    _____

Do Life In Community

5. Make it a point this week to share with someone the highlights of what you learned in this series.

Be On Mission

6. Reflect and meditate this week on Revelation 22:16-17. Let these verses of invitation motivate you to share the love of Christ and the hope of Heaven with people you care about.

Small Group
Leader Resources

THE
REAL
HEAVEN
What the Bible Actually Says

Group Agreement

People come to groups with a variety of expectations. The purpose of a group agreement is simply to make sure everyone is on the same page and that we have some common expectations.

The following Group Agreement is a tool to help you discuss specific guidelines during your first meeting. Modify anything that does not work for your group, then be sure to discuss the questions in the section called Our Game Plan. This will help you to have an even greater group experience.

We Agree to the Following Priorities

- Take the Bible Seriously — To seek to understand and apply God's truth in the Bible.

- Group Attendance — To give priority to the group meeting. I will call if I am going to be absent or late.

- Safe Environment — To create a safe place where people can be heard and feel loved. There are no snap judgments or simple fixes.

- Respectful Discussion — To speak in a respectful and honoring way to others in the group.

- Be Confidential — To keep anything that is shared strictly confidential and within the group.

- Spiritual Health — To give group members permission to help me live a godly, healthy spiritual life that is pleasing to God.

- Building Relationships — To get to know the other members of the group and pray for them regularly.

- Pursue B.I.O. — To encourage and challenge each other in coming "before God" daily, doing life together "in community", and being "on mission" 24/7.

- Prayer — To regularly pray with and for each other.

- Other

_____

_____

Our Game Plan

1. What day and time will we meet?

   _____

   _____

   _____

2. Where will we meet?

   _____

   _____

   _____

3. How long will we meet each week?

   _____

   _____

   _____

4. What will we do for refreshments?

   _____

   _____

   _____

5. What will we do about childcare?

   _____

   _____

   _____

THE **REAL HEAVEN**
What the Bible Actually Says

How to Make This a Meaningful Experience for Your Group

Before the Group Arrives

1. **Be prepared.** Your personal preparation can make a huge difference in the quality of the group experience. We strongly suggest previewing both the DVD teaching by Chip Ingram and the study guide.

2. **Pray for your group members by name.** Ask God to use your time together to touch the heart of every person in your group. Expect God to challenge and change people as a result of this study.

3. **Provide refreshments.** There's nothing like food to help a group relax and connect with each other. For the first week, we suggest you prepare a snack. After that, ask other group members to bring the food so that they share in the responsibilities of the group and make a commitment to return.

4. **Relax.** Don't try to imitate someone else's style of leading a group. Lead the group in a way that fits your style and temperament. Remember that people may feel nervous showing up for a small group study, so put them at ease when they arrive. Make sure to have all the details covered prior to your group meeting, so that once people start arriving, you can focus on them.

Group Meeting Format

Take It In (Watch the video)

1. **Get the video ready.** Each video session on the DVD will have three components. First, Chip will spend a few minutes introducing this week's topic. Next, you will watch the content that Chip taught in front of a live audience—this portion of the video will be roughly 25-30 minutes in length. Lastly, Chip will share some closing thoughts and set up the discussion time for your group.

2. **Have ample materials.** Before you start the video, make sure everyone has their own copy of the study guide. Encourage the group to open to this week's session and follow along with the teaching. There is an outline in the study guide with an opportunity to fill in the outline.

3. **Arrange the room.** Set up the chairs in the room so that everyone can see the television. Arrange the room in such a way that it is conducive to discussion.

Talk It Over

Here are some guidelines for leading the discussion time:

1. **Make this a discussion, not a lecture.** Resist the temptation to do all the talking and to answer your own questions. Don't be afraid of a few moments of silence while people formulate their responses.

   Don't feel like you need to have all the answers. There is nothing wrong with simply saying, "I don't know the answer to that, but I'll see if I can find an answer this week."

2. **Encourage everyone to participate.** Don't let one person dominate, but also don't pressure quieter members to speak. Be patient. Ask, good follow-up questions, and be sensitive to delicate issues.

3. **Affirm people's participation and input.** If an answer is clearly wrong, ask "What led you to that conclusion?" or ask what the rest of the group thinks. If a disagreement arises, don't be too quick to shut it down. The discussion can draw out important perspectives. If you still can't resolve a disagreement, offer to research it further and return to the issue next week.

   However, if someone goes on the offensive and engages in personal attacks, you will need to step in as the leader. In the midst of spirited discussion, we must also remember that people are fragile and there is no place for disrespect.

4. **Detour when necessary.** If an important question is raised that is not in the study guide, take time to discuss it. Also, if someone shares something personal and emotional, take time for him or her. Stop and pray for him or her right then. Allow the Holy Spirit room to maneuver, and follow His prompting when the discussion changes direction.

5. **Subgroup.** One of the principles of small group life is "when numbers go up, sharing goes down." If you have a large group, sometimes you may want to split up into groups of 4-6 people for the discussion time. This is a great way to give everyone, even the quieter members, a chance to share. Choose someone in the group to guide each of the smaller groups through the discussion. This involves others in the leadership of the group and provides an opportunity for training new leaders.

6. **Pray.** Be sensitive to the fact that some people in your group may be uncomfortable praying out loud. As a general rule, don't call on people to pray unless you have asked them ahead of time or have heard them pray in public. But this can also be a time to help people build their confidence to pray in a group. Consider having prayer times that ask people to just say a word or sentence of thanks to God.

Live It Out – B.I.O.

Bio is a word that is synonymous with "life." Found in those three simple letters — B.I.O. — is the key to helping you become the person God wants you to be.

B = Come "Before God" daily

Meet with Him personally through prayer and His Word to enjoy His presence, receive His direction, and follow His will.

I = Do Life "In Community" weekly

Structure your week to personally connect in safe relationships that provide love, support, transparency, challenge, and accountability.

O = Be "On Mission" 24/7

Cultivate a mindset to live out Jesus' love for others through acts of sacrifice as well as service at home, work, play, and church.

Accelerate (20 minutes that turn concepts into convictions)

Inspiration comes from hearing God's Word. **Motivation** grows by discussing God's Word. **Transformation** occurs when you study it for yourself.

If you want to "accelerate" your growth, here is an assignment you can do at home each week. Our convictions become even stronger when we dig into Scripture and discover truth for ourselves. To help you get the most out of this exercise, consider partnering up with someone in your group who will also commit to do the assignment this week. Then, after you have each completed the assignment, agree to spend 10 minutes by phone sharing what you learned and what you are applying.

Session Notes

Thanks for hosting this series on Heaven. You are going to discover that the Bible has a lot more to say about Heaven than you think. Whether you are brand new at leading a small group or you are a seasoned veteran, God is going to use you. God has a long history of using ordinary people to get His work done.

These brief notes are intended to help prepare you for each week's session. By spending just a few minutes each week previewing the video and going over these session notes, you will set the table for a great group experience. Also, don't forget to pray for your group each week.

Session 1 — Why Heaven Matters, Pt. 1

- If your group doesn't know each other well, be sure that you spend some time getting acquainted. Don't rush right into the video lesson. Remember, small groups are not just about a study or a meeting, they are about relationships.

- Be sure to capture everyone's contact information. It is a good idea to send out an email with everybody's contact information so that the group can stay in touch. At the back of your study guide is a roster where people can fill in the names and contact information of the other group members.

- When you are ready to start the session, be sure that each person in your group has a copy of the study guide. The small group study guide is important for people to follow along and to take notes.

- Spend a little time in this first session talking about B.I.O. These three core practices are the pathway to maturity. You will see these letters and terms throughout this curriculum. Start getting your group comfortable with the concepts of "coming before God," "doing life together in community," and "being on mission."

- One of the statements Chip is going to make is that "our faulty view of Heaven destines us to a wasted life here on earth." That is a strong statement. Discussion question #4 flows out of Chip's statement. Be sure your group spends some time engaging this question.

- Sometimes Chip will ask you as the facilitator to lead the way by answering the first question. This allows you to lead by example, and your willingness to share openly about your life will help others feel the permission to do the same.

- Before you wrap up your group time, be sure to introduce the Accelerate exercise in the study guide. This is an assignment they can do during the week that will help turbo charge their growth. Encourage them to find a partner in the group who they can talk to each week about the Accelerate exercise.

Session 2 — Why Heaven Matters, Pt. 2

- Why not begin your preparation by praying right now for the people in your group. You might even want to keep their names in your Bible. You may also want to ask people in your group how you can pray for them specifically.

- If somebody doesn't come back this week, be sure and follow up with him or her. Even if you knew him or her were going to have to miss the group meeting, give him or her a call or shoot him or her an email letting him or her know that he or she were missed. It would also be appropriate to have a couple of other people in the group let him or her know he or she were missed.

- If you haven't already previewed the video, take the time to do so. It will help you know how to best facilitate the group and what are the best discussion questions for your group.

- This week Chip will close the session by talking about three practical implications of an accurate view of Heaven.

- Perspective in times of trouble?

- Perseverance in times of temptation?… or

- Priorities when under pressure?

  He will launch your group into discussion by asking, "Which of those three statements most connects with you personally?" Give that question some thought ahead of time. If you have a personal story to share from your own life, that would be great.

- As you walk your group through this study, keep coming back to this fundamental question: "How does this study about Heaven impact and inform how we live on earth?"

Session 3 — What's Heaven Like?, Pt. 1

- Did anybody miss last week's session? If so, make it a priority to follow up and let him or her know he or she were missed. It just might be your care for him or her that keeps him or her connected to the group.

- Share the load. One of the ways to raise the sense of ownership within the group is to get them involved in more than coming to the meeting. So, get someone to help with refreshments... find somebody else to be in charge of the prayer requests... get someone else to be in charge of any social gathering you plan... let someone else lead the discussion one night. Give away as much of the responsibility as possible. That is GOOD leadership.

- Think about last week's meeting for a moment. Was there anyone that didn't talk or participate? In every group, there are extroverts and there are introverts. There are people who like to talk and then there are those who are quite content NOT to talk. Not everyone engages in the same way or at the same level but you do want to try and create an environment where everyone wants to participate.

- During this week's session, Chip will talk about the Rapture, the Tribulation, and the Great White Throne Judgment. There are a lot of different opinions about these events. If you will watch the coaching video this week, Chip will give you some practical coaching for how to handle discussing these coming events.

- Follow up with your group this week to see how they did with the Accelerate assignment this week. Don't shame or embarrass anyone who didn't get to the assignment, but honestly challenge him or her to make this a priority in the coming week.

Session 4 — What's Heaven Like?, Pt. 2

- You are now at the halfway point of this series. How is it going? How well is the group connecting? What has been going well and what needs a little work? Are there any adjustments you need to make?

- Don't feel any pressure to get through all the questions. As people open up and talk, don't move on too quickly. Give them the space to consider what is going on inside them as they interact with this teaching.

- Don't be afraid of silence. When you ask people a question, give them time to think about it. Don't feel like you have to fill every quiet moment with words.

- One way to deepen the level of community within your group is to spend time together outside the group meeting. If you have not already done so, plan something that will allow you to get to know each other better. Also, consider having someone else in the group take responsibility for your fellowship event.

- You might want to have a couple of extra Bibles available this week. Chip is going to give you a lot of Scripture references in this week's lesson. Don't be afraid to spend some time looking up those passages in your discussion time.

Session 5 — A New Home for the New You, Pt. 1

- Confidentiality is crucial to group life. The moment trust is breached, people will shut down and close up. So, you may want to mention the importance of confidentiality again this week just to keep it on people's radar.

- Each time your group meets, take a few minutes to update everyone on what has happened since the last group meeting. Ask people what they are learning and putting into practice. Remember, being a disciple of Jesus means becoming a "doer of the Word."

- Revisit the importance of B.I.O. this week. Reinforce the importance of people integrating these core practices in their lives. For example, talk about the priority of coming before God each day and submitting to the authority of God's truth.

- We are just sessions away from completing this series. This would be a good week to talk about finishing strong and also what your group is going to do after this series. As a group, you may want to get out a computer and go to LivingontheEdge.org and look at all the small group curriculums that are available.

- In the first discussion question this week, Chip will ask those in your group to "Share about a time in their life when they really 'thirsted' for (wanted) something… and then when they got it, it just didn't satisfy like they thought it would." This is a great opportunity for you as the leader to have an example from your life. Share honestly and transparently.

Session 6 — A New Home for the New You, Pt. 2

- Take a few minutes this week before you get into the study to talk about the impact of this series. Ask people what they are learning and how it is impacting their lives.

- Be sure that everyone is clear what your group is doing next after this study.

- As this series winds down, this is a good time to plan some kind of party or fellowship after you complete the study. Find the "party person" in your group and ask him or her to take on the responsibility of planning a fun experience for the group. Also, use this party as a time for people to share how God has used this series to grow them and change them.

- At the end of this week's session, Chip will clearly and powerfully share the gospel. A study on Heaven confronts all of us with our mortality and the fact that this life is not all there is. Chip will lead people through a prayer giving them the opportunity to receive Christ. Don't assume that everybody in your group has made that decision. After Chip prays, let your group know that if anybody prayed that prayer, that you would love to talk to him or her after the session.

- If someone did receive Christ, point him or her to the LivingontheEdge. org website to find help for getting started in his or her faith

- Also near the end of the session, Chip will ask those of us who are believers if we have friends and family and co-workers who don't know Christ. And he will challenge us to be the ones to boldly share the good news of Jesus with them. Spend some time talking about this with your group. Maybe even share names of people that you could pray for in your group meeting.

Prayer and Praise

One of the most important things you can do in your group is to pray with and for each other. Write down each other's concerns here so you can remember to pray for these requests during the week.

Use the Follow Up box to record an answer to prayer or to write down how you might want to follow up with the person making the request. This could be a phone call, an email, or a card. Your personal concern will mean a lot!

Date	Person	Prayer Request	Follow Up

Date	Person	Prayer Request	Follow Up

Date	Person	Prayer Request	Follow Up

Date	Person	Prayer Request	Follow Up

Date	Person	Prayer Request	Follow Up

Date	Person	Prayer Request	Follow Up

Date	Person	Prayer Request	Follow Up

Date	Person	Prayer Request	Follow Up

Date	Person	Prayer Request	Follow Up

Date	Person	Prayer Request	Follow Up

Date	Person	Prayer Request	Follow Up

Date	Person	Prayer Request	Follow Up

Date	Person	Prayer Request	Follow Up

Date	Person	Prayer Request	Follow Up

Date	Person	Prayer Request	Follow Up

Date	Person	Prayer Request	Follow Up

THE **REAL HEAVEN**
What the Bible Actually Says

Group Roster

Name	Home Phone	Email

Group Roster

Name	Home Phone	Email

Notes:

_____

_____

_____

_____

_____

_____

_____

_____

_____

_____

_____

_____

_____

_____

_____

_____

_____

_____

_____

_____

_____

_____

_____

_____

Notes:

Notes:

_____

_____

_____

_____

_____

_____

_____

_____

_____

_____

_____

_____

_____

_____

_____

_____

_____

_____

_____

_____

_____

What's Next?
More Group Bible Studies from Chip Ingram

Balancing Life's Demands
Biblical Priorities for a Busy Life
Busy, tired, and stressed out? Learn how to put first things first and find peace in the midst of pressure and adversity.

Culture Shock
A Biblical Response to Today's Most Divisive Issues
Bring light—not heat—to divisive issues, such as abortion, homosexuality, sex, politics, the environment, and more.

Doing Good
What Happens When Christians Really Live Like Christians
This series clarifies what Doing Good will do in you and then through you, for the benefit of others and the glory of God.

Experiencing God's Dream for Your Marriage
Practical Tools for a Thriving Marriage
Examine God's design for marriage and the real-life tools and practices that will transform it for a lifetime.

Watch previews and order at
LivingontheEdge.org
or 888.333.6003.

What's Next?
More Group Bible Studies from Chip Ingram

The Real God
How He Longs for You to See Him

A deeper look at seven attributes of God's character that will change the way you think, pray, and live.

Good to Great in God's Eyes
10 Practices Great Christians Have in Common

If you long for spiritual breakthrough, take a closer look at ten powerful practices that will rekindle a fresh infusion of faith.

The Real Heaven
What the Bible Actually Says

Chip Ingram digs into Scripture to reveal what heaven will be like, what we'll do there, and how we're to prepare for eternity today.

Holy Ambition
Turning God-Shaped Dreams Into Reality

Do you long to turn a God-inspired dream into reality? Learn how God uses everyday believers to accomplish extraordinary things.

The Invisible War
The Believer's Guide to Satan, Demons, and Spiritual Warfare
Learn how to clothe yourself with God's spiritual armor and be confident of victory over the enemy of your soul.

Love, Sex and Lasting Relationships
God's Prescription to Enhance Your Love Life
Do you believe in true love? Discover a better way to find love, stay in love, and build intimacy that lasts a lifetime.

Overcoming Emotions That Destroy
Constructive Tools for Destructive Emotions
We all struggle with destructive emotions that can ruin relationships. Learn God's plan to overcome angry feelings for good.

Transformed
The Miracle of Life Change
Ready to make a change? Explore God's process of true transformation and learn to spot barriers that hold you back from receiving God's best.

True Spirituality
Becoming a Romans 12 Christian
We live in a world that is activity-heavy and relationship-light. Learn the next steps toward True Spirituality.

Why I Believe
Straight Answers to Honest Questions about God, the Bible and Christianity
Can miracles be explained? Is there really a God? There are solid, logical answers about claims of the Christian faith.

Your Divine Design
Discover, Develop, and Deploy Your Spiritual Gifts
How has God uniquely wired you? Discover God's purpose for spiritual gifts and how to identify your own.

Download the Chip Ingram App

The Chip Ingram App delivers daily devotionals, broadcasts, message notes, blog articles, and more right on your mobile device.